I0473845

Copyright © Kristina Pawliw. All rights reserved. Permission must be obtained to reproduce whole or part of this publication.

Disclaimer:

The contents of this book are the honest opinion of the author and do not constitute professional advice. In no event shall the author be liable for any outcomes arising from using the information in this book.

Fictitious names and scenarios have been used throughout. Any resemblance to actual persons, living or deceased, is purely coincidental.

Building sustainable capacity

Introduction

Developing sustainable capacity is like growing a garden. You need to plant the seeds, water and feed them, then wait for them to sprout. Once they do, you need to train the plants to grow upwards, remove weeds and tend them regularly. When you garden, you know that the plant will eventually grow- even though at the beginning nothing seems to be happening. You don't go uprooting the seeds during that time- you wait patiently for the results you know will occur in time. You also know that you can't do the work for the seed- you can help it along, but it needs to grow on its own.

This book is like a gardening manual for the capacity developer. It outlines, in practical terms, the 'seasons' of Capacity Development and what to expect and do in each one. By following the steps you will see results- just like a seasoned gardener.

What is Capacity Development ?

The Chinese proverb "Give a man a fish and you feed him for a day. Teach a man to fish and you feed him for a lifetime" is an apt description for Capacity Development.

Capacity Development involves teaching others to 'fish' for themselves, so they may pass the knowledge on and become self-sufficient. Although it may sound counter-intuitive, the ultimate aim of Capacity Development is to "do yourself out of a job". Whether that happens quickly, or over generations, depends on the environment.

The staircase analogy

Imagine you have to build a set of stairs. You start from the bottom and build the first step as a solid foundation. Once that is strong you build the second, and so on, until your reach the top. The same approach applies to Capacity Development. Build the first step- your foundation- and make sure it is solid. Then build the next steps one at a time, progressively. The time you take for each step can vary -and you may not be able to build the whole staircase during your term.

Before any building work begins, plans must be drawn up. You take accurate measurements of the gap between the floors and work out how many steps are required. You measure the materials so they fit together. Building capacity is similar- you need to work out what gap there is between where you are and where you need to go (identify the *Capacity Development gaps*) and what materials to use and how they will fit together (the *Capacity Development plan*). And like a staircase, your Capacity Development should be solid when complete and all support is removed (or be sustainable). This result is what I call *sustainable Capacity Development.*

Doing v teaching

Many Capacity Development programmes select experts in various fields-however I noticed that the most successful capacity developers were those with technical expertise in addition to what are known as 'soft' skills- such as the ability to communicate with people who have a lower skill base compared to you.

Some of the best tips I gained to help me were from a teacher. She helped me understand how people learn best, and how to make learning interesting. You don't need to be a teacher, though to build good capacity- but taking a similar approach helps develop a rich learning experience for your counterparts. Think back to your own experience in the classroom- did you find it interesting when someone spoke at you, or when someone told you an interesting story with a lesson? When you practiced something or were told how it should work?

Be honest about your ability to work autonomously

Capacity Development is hard work. It tests and pushes you. Often you will be on your own in challenging circumstances- without the luxury of colleagues to run things by. You may find yourself in delicate, high-stake situations requiring an immediate response, or having to make unpopular decisions. You may also have to 'fight' for resources.

So if you haven't had to make tough decisions, negotiate and defend a position for resources and projects, or made an unpopular decision to get a job done properly- then it may be a good idea to get some experience in these areas before doing a capacity building role which is highly autonomous. A great way to start in this field if you haven't had much experience in a leadership role is working with a program that is headed by an experienced team leader, and where you are part of a team of capacity developers in an organisation. This approach enables provides you with much needed support and guidance to negotiate the challenges of working in a Capacity Development environment.

The golden rules

Believe in your counterparts

The central tenet to being successful in Capacity Development is believing in your counterparts. If you don't have faith in them, then why should they trust you to help them? Why would they go out of their comfort zone for someone who doesn't think they can do it?

Respect your counterparts

We have all experienced obnoxious travellers who loudly complain that nothing is as good as it is at home. Keep that image in mind when you start in your new organisation. Although you may have significant expertise, always respect the experiences of your counterparts. I remember hearing an awful story about a young capacity developer meeting a counterpart in a public place. She was pointing her finger at her counterpart, who was senior to her in age and rank, and telling him he did not know what he was doing. Her counterpart was sitting back, not saying a word, but with a blank look on his face. How do you think she went in getting support for her Capacity Development initiatives after that?

Be consistently positive

When you are developing skills you need the patience of a teacher. Your counterparts will look to you for inspiration and support to make shifts in behaviour and skills. You will need to be their champion and keep them on track. To do this over a long period of time requires you to nurture yourself by taking regular breaks, working sensible hours and having a strong support network. It is very easy to fall into the trap of working long hours because there is so much to do, but remember you are doing a marathon and not a sprint. You need to be able to make it over the long run- burning out part way through doesn't help anyone.

Keep a long-term view and hold the vision for your counterparts

In most cases, it takes time to develop skills. Ensure you have that firmly in your mind and that your counterparts understand the timeframe, too, so they do not become disheartened. Like anyone learning new skills they will not be perfect the first time they try. By holding the vision of where they are aiming to be during times when things aren't going so well, you will help them get back up and try again. And that consistency is the way to achieve results.

For example, Tim had been in his role as a budget adviser for two years. He had worked hard with his counterparts over the last two years to reform the budget so the Department could receive additional funding from the national Treasury. Although the Department had received good feedback from Treasury on the improvements, significant funding increases were yet to be seen. Tim's counterparts were beginning to lose heart, and it took some motivating to encourage them to submit another big effort for this year's budget. He reminded them that they were looking for long term gains from their efforts- so they should not be discouraged if they did not receive instant results. With a lot of encouragement, his counterparts did submit a budget that was even better than their last effort. And they were rewarded with an unprecedented 20% jump in funding.

The important thing Tim did here was to keep his team focussed on the prize. He held the long-term vision for his team when they had doubts. As a Capacity Developer this is one of your most important roles as it provides that solid foundation of support your counterparts can rely on. This is vitally important in environments where the staff have little support from their organisation. It is tiring, and gets harder to do the longer you are in a role.

Speak their language

By this, I do not mean speak Urdu if that is the native tongue of your counterparts. Instead, use metaphors, phrases and sayings which resonate with the interests of your counterparts.

For instance, Jillian's counterpart Fred loves American football. To 'speak his language', she uses phrases such as 'game-plan', 'touch-down' and 'last quarter'.

This technique does a few things. Firstly, it makes it easier for your counterpart to understand your message. It is also more meaningful to them, as you are referring to something they are interested in. This makes it far more likely your message will 'stick' in the mind of your counterpart. It is also a powerful way to build rapport.

Challenges

Expect push back

Capacity Development is a very profitable industry for consulting firms and project managers. Is it in their interest to build sustainable capacity? Not really. But it is in the interest of the Capacity Development recipient to become self-sufficient so they can effectively operate their own organisations and train others to do the same. Having a strong partner also provides donors with benefits such as money and time that can be spent in other, more pressing areas.

The concept of sustainable Capacity Development can meet resistance from Capacity Development recipients, particularly if they had work done for them by other Capacity Development advisers.

For example, Jennifer asked a counterpart to draft a document, based on a template she provided and after walking the counterpart through how it should be done. Her counterpart listened politely, then retired to her office. Jennifer heard from another counterpart that this lady complained "why can't Jennifer do it?" and comment that Jennifer's predecessor had done this work for her. Rather than talk to her counterpart about it, Jennifer just waited for a week and followed up on the counterpart's progress. Jennifer was not surprised to find that nothing had been done. Jennifer sat down with her again and asked what she was having trouble with. This helped identify that her counterpart did not have the confidence to write. With some gentle encouragement, Jennifer's counterpart presented her with a draft document the next day, and glowed with pride when Jennifer told her the draft was good. This set the foundation for her counterpart being promoted into a management position, which involved a large amount of report writing.

Being tested

You may hear stories about the things your predecessor did for your counterparts. This is a natural way of dealing with change, so don't take it personally. The way you handle this will play a big part in the way your counterparts view you. By being graceful and not letting your ego get hooked you will engender trust and respect. What worked for me was to just listen, acknowledge the feelings expressed to me- and nothing more. No questioning of the sentiments or trying to convince my counterparts of a different perspective. By accepting the situation and not trying to fight it, I found it stopped relatively quickly and my counterparts respected that I had let them express their feelings without judging them or trying to convince them of an alternate view.

Conflicting loyalties

The longer you are in a Capacity Development role, particularly where you are embedded in an organisation- the more strongly you will identify with your counterparts. You may experience conflicting loyalties between the expectations of your boss, and those of your counterparts. Having a clearly defined Capacity Development plan and referring back to that in situations of conflicts of interest is a good first step. Another is to refer back to the strategic aims of the program that both your boss and your counterparts have signed up to. Colleagues in your program can be an invaluable source of support and guidance, and a good sounding board in such situations.

Be aware of 'improvement fatigue'

We all have a limit for how much self-development we can sustain before we begin to feel tired and overwhelmed. This phenomenon is what I call 'improvement fatigue'. Pushing ahead with Capacity Development activities when your counterparts feel like this is counterproductive.

When that point is reached, focus on spending time with your counterparts and begin Capacity Development activities again when they are ready.

I have not suggested any timeframes for reaching 'fatigue point' or the rest period between capacity building as this differs between organisations and depends on many different variables. It is something you will need to determine by observation and 'trial and error'. To assist with this determination, it may help to talk with your counterparts to develop an understanding of the way they work best.

Stages and timeframe

The typical length of time for many Capacity Development program contracts is three years, which is the timeframe used in this book.

Within a 3 year timeframe, there are five distinct timeframes-or natural progressions - that I noticed:

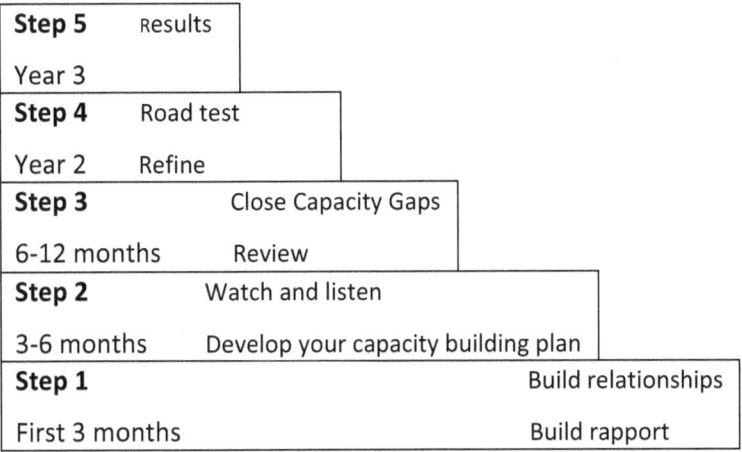

Step 5	Results	
Year 3		
Step 4	Road test	
Year 2	Refine	
Step 3	Close Capacity Gaps	
6-12 months	Review	
Step 2	Watch and listen	
3-6 months	Develop your capacity building plan	
Step 1		Build relationships
First 3 months		Build rapport

As every situation is unique, these time frames are best used as a guide. They can also be applied to shorter or longer Capacity Development terms by contracting or extending the timeframes commensurately.

Step 1: First 3 months

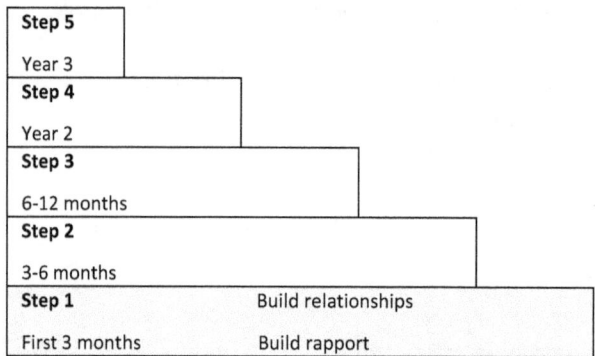

Step 5	
Year 3	
Step 4	
Year 2	
Step 3	
6-12 months	
Step 2	
3-6 months	
Step 1	Build relationships
First 3 months	Build rapport

Build relationships

Your aim in this period is to create a fertile garden bed for your capacity building 'garden' to grow.

Welcome calls

When you first arrive in your Capacity Development role, you may receive a polite but distant welcome. It may also take a few months before anyone will come to you. If this happens, don't panic!

If you haven't already, your first step should be a round of visits to key people in your organisation and with external stakeholders. The purpose of these calls is to introduce yourself and let your counterparts know how to contact you. You may find your host discusses issues he or she would like your assistance with. At first it may be quite challenging to work out how the information fits together- this will get easier as you become more familiar with the organisation. If appropriate, you may wish to extend and invitation to visit your office- this helps build rapport and reduce any mystery about where you work and what you do.

Familiarisation visits

Get out and visit all relevant sites of your host organisation as soon as possible. This enables you to learn about the organisation and understand the concerns of your counterparts. It is a vital component of relationship development if you are in a geographically dispersed organisation, especially if technology does not support good communication. If you can fund one of your counterparts to travel with you from your Capacity Development budget, this is a great way to be introduced to colleagues in different locations and also gives your counterpart an opportunity to exchange information with their colleagues. This becomes particularly important where an organisation has limited funds for your counterparts to visit outlying parts of the organisation.

Daily 'floor walks' with your counterparts

Sitting behind a desk or in an office may get work done-but that is not the aim of the game in Capacity Development. By walking around the offices or desks of counterparts each day, you will build relationships and also understand what their working environment and challenges are. Consistency is essential. Taking the time to do this each day will reap you rewards in terms of people feeling they can trust you- although it may take time to manifest.

For example, Gina made sure she said hello to everyone she met and took the time to chat- about anything. She showed interest in the person- not for their position or how they could help achieve capacity building results. Gina had one counterpart who would not speak to her, or address her by name when talking about her to others. Gina made sure she said hello every time she saw him and asked him how he was. After 6 months, he felt comfortable enough to attend one of Gina's training sessions. After 18 months, he would say hello back to Gina when she greeted him, and call her by her name. Gina was so excited the first time he did this, as it showed that by being patient and consistent she had made inroads and developed the relationship. Whilst this may seem like a small step compared to other shifts in capacity, it was one of the most meaningful for Gina.

Another example is a counterpart of Jack's who was in charge of a key division. He was a hard man to get a meeting with. Jack tried for a year and a half through various means, but was not successful. Then, in year three, he agreed to meet with Jack to plan a budget. When help was required to get work done by the budget deadline, Jack pitched in to help him. The result of this collaboration was that his counterpart got funding where none was provided the year before, which Jack's counterpart was grateful for. Jack's counterpart now trusted him enough to work with him on a highly successful reform program- one which would not have been possible without Jack's counterpart's support.

Be a good host

An extension of the above is to have an open door policy and show consistent hospitality. If you have an office, have tea and coffee facilities and supplies and ensure you invite people for a chat and morning tea. If you don't have your own office, take your counterparts out for coffee or lunch. By creating an informal environment you can get to know your counterparts better and may find you get better work results when talking through issues in this setting, too. You may find you spend a fair amount much of your week doing this but it is a worthwhile investment.

Socialise with stakeholders

Those in diplomatic roles know that a lot of work gets done in social situations- and Capacity Development is very similar.

It is crucial to your ability to work successfully with your stakeholders that you build relationships outside work to do your job effectively. Think of it as your 'second' job. You may also find that you meet people who will be helpful to your work that you would not otherwise come across- especially in smaller communities.

For example, Sharna's organisation hosted a monthly morning tea. Even though this conflicted with another stakeholder meeting, Sharna attended each one and got to know counterparts in different divisions. As a result, she met Betty, the assistant to her host Department's Secretary. Six months later, Sharna needed to see the Secretary urgently- and with Betty's help, she obtained a timely appointment. In contrast, her predecessor had not been able to secure an appointment with the Secretary for 2 years.

Build rapport

Rapport is about connection. Techniques such as active listening, reframing, and emphasising similarities are key ways to build strong connections.

Active listening

When you are focussed completely on what the speaker is saying- not thinking about your shopping list or what you will say next, you are listening actively. This helps you to focus on what your speaker is saying, rather than trying to remember it all and plan what you will say next. A helpful technique is to wait until the speaker has finished talking, and frame a question based on the last thing they said to you.

Emphasise similarities

When you feel you have something in common with someone, you are more likely to feel comfortable with them and consider them an ally. This is the sort of view you want your counterparts to have of you. Sometimes it may be difficult to find similarities given your differing experiences and backgrounds. But some basic areas of common ground can include:

- experiences with family

- the challenges of balancing work and home life

- challenges with siblings/raising children

- difficulties with a boss

- sport

- *for female counterparts*: an interest in people and feeling good- be it through reading magazines, sharing books or newspaper articles.

If in doubt, observing your counterparts' topics of conversation can give you some clues.

It pays to keep an open mind in this respect. For instance, I would bring in general interest magazines and distribute them to the ladies in my team. One day, one of my male national colleagues saw one on my desk and asked if he could borrow it. I then noticed other males in the division reading it too. I had assumed, incorrectly, that men would not be interested in reading them. After expanding the distribution of the magazines to my male colleagues they would engage me in conversation about topical issues raised in the magazine. I had just discovered a Capacity Building tool that was effective and engaging for my particular counterparts.

Step 2: 3-6 months

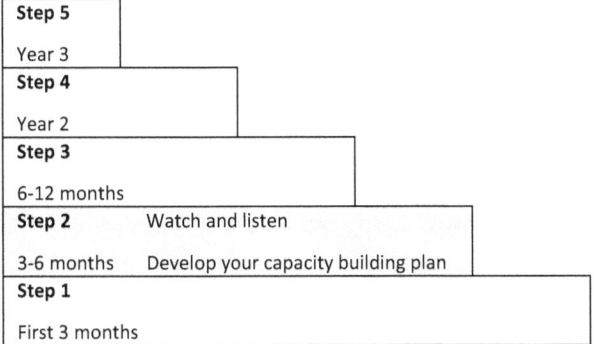

Step 5	
Year 3	
Step 4	
Year 2	
Step 3	
6-12 months	
Step 2	Watch and listen
3-6 months	Develop your capacity building plan
Step 1	
First 3 months	

At this point in time, you are in the cultivation rather than the 'reaping what you sow' or results stage.

Watch and listen

The best advice I received was to not make any changes or implement anything new for the first 6 months. Focus on understanding the environment, politics, personalities and issues of your host organisation so you that you can determine what the *Capacity Development gaps* are and come up with a Capacity Development plan that is achievable. Your counterparts will appreciate this as it shows you are genuinely interested in them and their issues.

Be aware that some aid programs or donors may want to see results during this stage. If you find yourself in this position, please refer to the *review* section of Stage 3.

Develop your capacity building plan

Whilst you can come up with a draft based on your observations, you are likely to get better results if you hold formal 'focus' groups with your counterparts. This highlights the participatory aspect of developing the plan, making it more likely to be supported by your counterparts.

Once you have come up with the plan, have it formally signed by you/your program manager and your host organisation. This further solidifies your host organisation's engagement with the process. If possible, have a formal 'unveiling' of the plan with a morning tea and short presentation of the plan, and distribute hard copies. By taking time out to celebrate the achievement and communicate the approach you will help cement the sense of mutual collaboration towards Capacity Development goals. And you may sow the seeds for unexpected results. For example, when Beth hosted a morning tea for an information session and distribution of her host organisation's Capacity Development plan, she was greeted by counterparts she had not met yet- because they didn't know she was there. They had heard 'on the grapevine' about the morning tea from a counterpart of Beth's so had come along to see what was going on and enjoy the cake. It turned out that despite her best efforts and those of her the counterparts in her division, she had not been advised (or yet discovered) a division in the organisation that was crucial to her plan being achieved. Beth set up a meeting with this newly discovered colleague which set the stage for future Capacity Development activities.

What is a Capacity Development plan?

Basically, your Capacity Development plan will list the areas which need to be worked on so the organisation can meet its objectives. These objectives may be set by government or for private organisations, by shareholders or in business plans. If you are working under an aid program your plan will also be influenced by the objectives of that program, host organisation, and host and donor governments.

Think of your Capacity Development plan as a series of steps- in some areas you may be on the first step and only able to go up one step in 3 years. In other areas you may be at the middle of the staircase and jump up 2 steps in six months.

Key Capacity Development plan components

So, what should a Capacity Development plan include?

Whilst many Capacity Development programmes have tailored Capacity Development plan templates, as a guide, the basics are:

- Capacity gap

- How to close the gap

- Timeframe for doing so

- Who does what

- How results will be measured.

When should it be prepared?

Some programs seek a Capacity Development plan in the first month. I suggest it is more realistic to do this at the six month stage, after you have had sufficient time to develop an understanding of the organisation. If this is not likely to be supported and you have an option to choose the timing of your Capacity Development plan, you may wish to consider a middle ground option- draft one after three months, to be reviewed at six months.

Capacity Development gap

Let's revisit the staircase analogy, which looks at sustainable capacity as the completed staircase. The gap between the first and second floors, (ie: where you are now in terms of capacity and where you need to go) is the

Capacity Development gap. Gaps are usually divided up by skill set or resource.

Some capacity gaps

Whilst every organisation is different, here are some general capacity gaps:

- Representational skills

- Management skills

- IT skills

- IT resources

- Financial management skills

- Customer service

- Managing workflow

- Progressing issues from start to finish

- Managing staff (particularly discipline)

- Presentation skills

- Writing skills

The 80/20 rule

A good rule of thumb in determining what to include in the plan is to use the 80/20 rule- pick the 20% of skills which will deliver 80% value. For example, if computer skills are low across the organisation and they are crucial to results, then focussing on improving them would deliver a big effect-so that would be a good *80%er*, so to speak. Another important factor is what is meaningful to the host organisation- if you pick an *80%er* that is not supported by the organisation, it's unlikely you will achieve it.

Closing capacity gaps

As a specialist in your area you are best placed to determine the types of activities that will help close the capacity gaps. Most organisations though will require regular training- both informal and formal. The training you provide need not cost anything- I developed my own training using readily available sources on the internet. Alternatively, you can arrange for counterparts to deliver 'peer-to-peer' training. Think about the training programs you have been on and what worked well- I am sure that being talked at for long periods was not something you enjoyed! So try and weave in things like videos, games, talks by experts, and using tools like books.

I have seen staff who attended many costly courses unable to translate that information back to their day-to-day work, rendering the training money ineffective. It highlighted for me that for learning to be solidified, it needs to be successfully translated into the workplace. I used mentoring to solidify any training. It is time consuming- but highly valuable and yields excellent results. For example, sitting with your counterparts and helping them set up their own budget spreadsheet is a good 'mentoring' approach to using excel and developing budgets. Another example is to have staff draft documents based on training in writing skills, for instance, then reviewing it with you. This approach also builds confidence in your counterparts as they are supported in trying something new. When the time comes to do the work on their own they are far more likely to be able to do so if you have taken a mentoring approach.

Step 3: 6-12 months

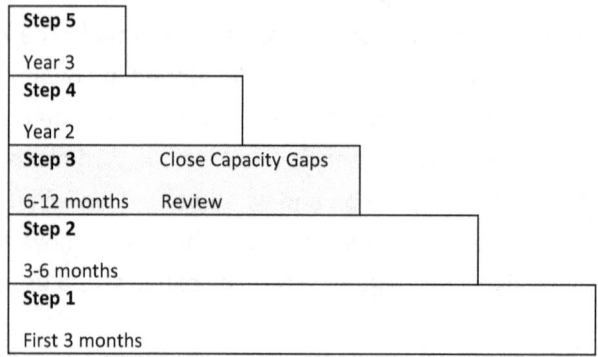

Step 5	
Year 3	
Step 4	
Year 2	
Step 3	Close Capacity Gaps
6-12 months	Review
Step 2	
3-6 months	
Step 1	
First 3 months	

In this phase the key focus is on working to close the capacity gaps. It is also the time you are likely to be asked to review and report on progress. Depending on the program, this is likely to be at the 6 to 12 month stage.

Review

Whilst ongoing review and adjustment of your Capacity Development plan is recommended, you will have formal review periods set by your program, donor, or host/donor government.

But I have no results to report! Does this mean I have failed to build capacity?

You are likely to notice your seeds are not yet sprouting in most areas of your Capacity Development 'garden' yet. If you think back to the analogy of a seed growing, you will recall that it is normal for a seed to have a germination period that looks like nothing is happening. Then all of a sudden, you see some small signs of life poking through the ground. In many countries, results take years, if not decades or generations to come to fruition- so remember that long-term view.

In a similar fashion, don't be discouraged if you are yet to see results from some or all of your Capacity Development areas. You can still report on progress- but in a different way. This is the time to note all the steps taken towards the goals- all the 'cultivating' that has been done. This will show your stakeholders the progress that has been made towards Capacity Development goals. Taking this approach will also show your counterparts that you believe in them and inspire them to keep on going despite the trials and tribulations. Remember that everything you do is noticed and either helps or hinders your progress towards Capacity Development goals- and the way you handle these reviews will be a key contributor to your success.

What should my review report look like?

Within the parameters set for you, keep your review templates as simple as possible so that your counterparts can understand them. To ensure results are formally accepted and notified to those who 'need to know', have the final version signed off by your host organisation and your program representative. Having a short information session to communicate the results to stakeholders is a great way to highlight key messages about progress to date, key challenges, and areas where further work is required.

Step 4: Year 2

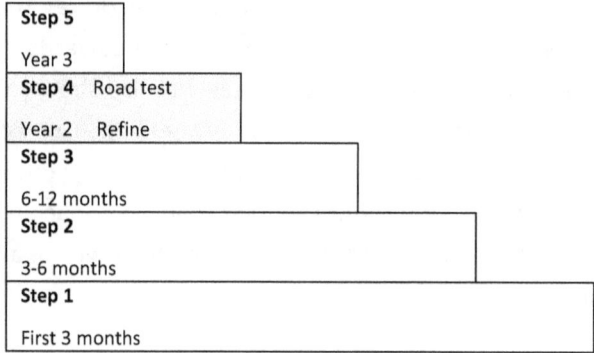

Road test and refine

Congratulations! You have made it to year two. This is when you road test your capacity develop plan and begin to see results. It is a very exciting time as you observe the groundwork you put into cultivating the garden bed finally begin to show results. It is also the time to refine your Capacity Development plan and either reduce the scope of activities to match where you are, or stretch them further.

You may observe you are learning more information as time passes, that either contradicts things you were told before or gives you a different spin on things. This is normal, and often occurs as you develop more solid relationships with your counterparts. Think of it like peeling away layers of an onion-except you are unlikely to ever get through all the layers!

For example, Kelly had spent the last two years in a Capacity Development role. One of her main activities was to develop the team's business plan with their involvement. After having one item on the plan for the last year, her counterparts told her that it wasn't really necessary. A new computer system had been implemented by a central agency that made it redundant. Kelly laughingly asked her counterparts why they had put the item on the business plan when it was not necessary. Her counterparts responded well to this relaxed and non-threatening approach, and explained that initially they were shy about revealing information to her in the first year. They also admitted that they lacked a full understanding of the implication of the system on their activities. Given that it was part of her counterparts' culture to 'save face' and take a long time to trust newcomers, Kelly realised just how far their relationship had developed if they were comfortable being this honest with her now. She acknowledged them for this, and as a result her counterparts felt they could trust her with the truth, whatever the implications. This deepened relationship helped refine the Capacity Development activities so that a majority of skills gaps were closed within her term.

Step 5: Year 3

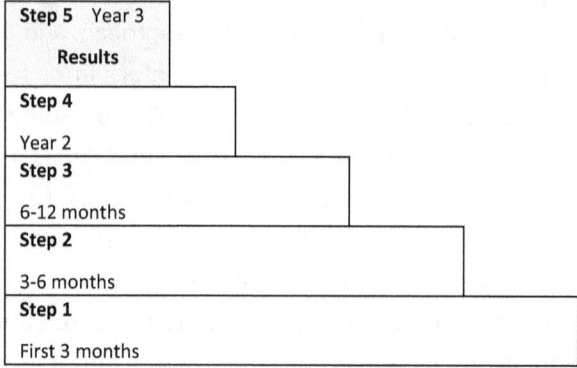

Results

This is when you really see the results of your efforts. If things have gone well you should see your counterparts displaying the skills you have built up in them over the past 2 years.

Make self-care more regular

After giving your energy consistently to others for three years, you may find your energy flagging far more easily in the third year. If so, take more frequent breaks to restore your energy levels.

There is a school of thought that suggests it is unwise to take back-to-back Capacity Development positions, as you do not get the opportunity to refresh your skills, and you run a higher risk of burn-out. Whilst this is dependant on many factors, it is always worth considering a break between Capacity Development roles to rest and retrain.

Start the year preparing for your departure

If you are coming to the end of your role at the end of year 3, it is important that you begin to prepare your colleagues for the fact they will

28

be working with someone new in the future, or that you may not be replaced. Funding for Capacity Development can never be guaranteed, and it is a good idea to make your Capacity Development partners aware of this possibility.

Some good tools to begin preparing in this year are plans for continuing major projects in future. It is also important that the small, everyday aspects you have assisted your counterparts with are documented. For example, Jerry prepared a stationery ordering and management plan to ensure that supplies were ordered in a timely fashion and distributed fairly in his organisation. Look closely at all the aspects you assist your counterparts with and ensure you have easy to understand guidance going forward.

To test the 'roadworthiness' of any such documents, you may wish to pass them out for comment and testing during the year so they can be adjusted and implemented whilst you can still provide guidance. This way, by the time you leave, the systems are up and running and familiar. Also, have them agreed to by the relevant stakeholders. By obtaining the input and agreement of your counterparts, the plans are far more likely to be utilised when you leave.

Schedule time for saying goodbye

During the last four to six weeks of your term, schedule time for saying goodbye to counterparts and stakeholders. In many cultures, farewell events are traditional and an important way of showing respect and gratitude. By ensuring your schedule accounts for this you can meet cultural expectations and enjoy the experience by making sure work is completed beforehand. Gift giving is central to many cultures, so be prepared with appropriate gifts for counterparts and stakeholders.

References

You may wish to consider giving references for counterparts, and may find yourself being asked for a few in your last few months.

Practical steps

This covers the little things like handing over the keys to your office; making sure it is left in good repair and clean condition; and ensuring that there are sufficient resources for anyone taking over from you.

What happens after year three?

Do you continue building increasing 'capacity' steps? Or do you rest a while at the top?

Many programs involve a change of Capacity Development staff at the end of a three year period. This does not mean that the Capacity Development ends, but that it is continued on, and hopefully the work done to date is built upon to develop a higher level of capacity.

However a change of personnel in a Capacity Development role can involve a backwards slide, as can a gap in Capacity Development assistance. It takes time to warm to a new person and depending on the culture, it can take months to years to develop sufficient rapport, trust and cultural understanding to begin developing capacity. It is wise to make allowances for this phenomenon during the first six months of any subsequent Capacity Development plans.

If you are being replaced, you may be involved in introducing your colleague to counterparts and stakeholders and handing over work. Handover notes are a great way of providing a handover if you are not meeting your replacement in person, and help provide a sense of continuity so that projects continue as smoothly as possible.

Finishing up

It is a sad and exciting time to come to the end of a Capacity Development journey. Sad, as you leave those you have worked alongside and shared so much with. Exciting, as you allow the structure you built to be tested by your absence.

In some cases, it can be frustrating to realise that goals set were not achieved, or that significant progress was not made. In these circumstances, remember that every journey begins with a single step. Your contribution is just one part of a long journey-and as such, it is valuable, important and relevant.

If you can, keep in touch with your counterparts after you leave. I have no doubt you will be thrilled with the examples of sustainable capacity they keep you informed of.

Being in a Capacity Development role is a true privilege. As you look back over your term, I hope you have as much to be proud of and grateful for as I did.

Glossary

Capacity Development gaps- the gap between the current skill level of counterparts/organisation and where they need to be for self-sufficiency.

Counterpart- the person/s you partner with to develop their skills. Usually refers to someone who is your rank or its equivalent in your host organisation. Sometimes ranks in public service organisations have similar names but are not equivalent.

Donor- the government or organisation providing the funding for the Capacity Development programme. Some programmes are funded by multiple donors.

Host organisation- the organisation you are working in as a Capacity Developer.

www.ingramcontent.com/pod-product-compliance
Lightning Source LLC
Chambersburg PA
CBHW071559170526
45166CB00004B/1717

* 9 7 8 1 4 7 5 2 2 8 3 8 0 *